Airlie Jane Kirkham

Music Stirs My Soul

© Airlie Jane Kirkham 2025

First published in July 2025 by immortalise
Hackham SA 5163
contact: info@immortalise.com.au

All rights reserved. Other than for the purposes and subject to the conditions prescribed under the Copyright Act, no part of this publication may be reproduced, stored in a retrieval system, or transmitted in any form or by any means, electronic, mechanical, photocopying, recording or otherwise, without the prior permission of the publisher.

ISBN 978-1-7638310-0-1

Poetry and musical compositions by Airlie Jane Kirkham.
Music by Pamela Kirkham and Katrina Rycroft
Artwork by Pamela Kirkham and Andrea Fidock.
Cover design and typesetting by Ben Morton.

Previously published by Airlie Jane Kirkham

There is A Light at the end of the Tunnel
　　　　　　　　　　　　　　– Ginninderra Press 2017

A Kaleidoscope of Paintings
　　　　　　　　　　　　　　– Ginninderra Press 2020

Sounds Around the River
　　　　　　　　　　　　　　– G.P 2018 Pocket Book

*by and for
Airlie
with love*

In memory of Airlie,

this is a collection of her poems,

musical compositions,

and some of her many achievements,

all told in her own words.

"MUSIC is my PASSION"

Contents

Acknowledgements viii

Foreword ix
    God's Gift of Words x
    Airlie's Testimony 1

SECTION ONE
Passion   5
    To Music 7
    Music is the Beat 9
    My Heart Rejoices 11
    Images of Music 13
    Music Today 15
    Minuet au Nouveau Classique 16
    Menuet in G 17
    Anecdote 18

SECTION TWO
Concerts and Operas   19
    An Opera House 21
    The Concert Hall 23
    Mahler in Concert 25
    An Afternoon with Airlie 27
    Thank You 29
    Japanese Song – Trio – Full Score 30
    Japanese Song – Piano 31
    Model of a Not-So-Modern Mother 32
    La Boheme 33

SECTION THREE
Sounds of Music   35
    River Sounds around the Paths 37
    Christmas Day 38
    Bells 39
    Morning Lark 40

The May Queen 41
Folk Dancing in the Abbey Books 42
The Church View 45
Memorials in Light 47
Unseen Memories 49
Sounds of Birds 51
Loch Lomond 52
Sounds of Creatures 54

SECTION FOUR
Poems and Music   55

Airlie's Invention 57
My Scholarship 58
My Destiny 59
Ode to Letho 60
Two Part Invention 61
Master of Music 62
Graduation Day 2/08/05 63
Two Part Invention 65
My OPERA Programmes 66
The second Program Opera in England 68
"Princess Airlie" 69
Funeral March Score 70
Charles Bodman Rae 71

Acknowledgements

This book honours the many aspects of music which gave Airlie opportunities to express her knowledge, feelings, and activities of music, where she gave her soul, mind, love and expression.

Airlie's mother, Pamela, who has been her amanuensis, guiding light and support for over 31 years since her tragic car accident in 1991, has produced this book.

Many thanks are extended to all to all her friends, mentors, Poetry Group "Poets of Passion" – to Alison, Dawn, Valerie, Ben and Jules who have edited and given good feedback to her.

Foreword

Airlie has always been interested in reading and writing poetry. She excelled at reading in primary school and explored poetry writing. Her first poem, written in infant school, was about a Green Frog. While at Secondary School, Woodlands C E G G S, Glenelg, Airlie won second prize in the annual State poetry writing competition. During this time, she also gained a B result in Australian Music Examinations Board eighth grade pianoforte.

Her love of Music led her to complete B.Mus. B.Mus. Hons. and after her accident, M.Mus. After this tragic car accident in 1991 and extended rehabilitation, she re-learnt to write in1998. Not surprisingly, her desire to write poetry again surfaced, and among her first writings were the words "I'm still here." It was clear that poetry and books still meant a lot to her, and from that time she has consistently written poems.

In 2002, she joined the group "Poets of Passion" and has continued to write ever since. Airlie needed her arm and hand supported to write so it was no easy task. Over the years her handwriting improved, and her poems displayed deep thinking and observations.

Pamela Kirkham (editor)

God's Gift of Words

We rely on the grace of God
for the gift of speech.
He nurtures us from infancy
as we attempt to speak.

I am ever thankful
for the gift of words,
a gift so precious,
a lifeblood to my whole being,
a lifeline to reach out
to every one of my friends and family.

My words are masterful.
I will use them to glorify God,
to tell others about God,
and to give Him praise.

Airlie's Testimony

I grew up in a Christian home and for that I am thankful. I had two sets of believing grandparents. Dad's parents were Salvation Army officers, living in Victoria, and Mum's were members of Holy Trinity Church, Adelaide. Poppa and Nanna were in the church choir and attended every week, and I recall Poppa singing me hymns he loved. Poppa died when I was four, so I don't remember him very much, but Nanna who lived to 104, became my mentor. She loved the Bible, particularly the 23rd Psalm. We enjoyed going to the opera together when I was grown up. Grandpa and Grandma lived in Melbourne, but they used to read the Bible to me when we were visiting them.

I went to Sunday School at Holy Trinity, and joined the youth fellowship when I was older. It was during these weekly gatherings, and our annual camps, that I came to realise for myself that God loved me so much. My parents had role modelled loving Christ, but I asked Jesus to come into my heart in these teen years, I put my whole trust in Him.

When I was at school, Woodlands, I also was influenced by Stewart, the school chaplain. After leaving school I went to the University of Adelaide where I joined the Evangelical Union. This exposure to people of my own age who were also Christians encouraged me to declare openly my faith. I went to the EU meetings and prayer groups, and attended the annual camp.

After I finished University, I had a job teaching at a church girls' school, and this gave me opportunities to share my love of Jesus with children. I also taught in Trinity Sunday School, and was a leader at Club 5-9, a school age group at church. When I had my accident in 1991, the love of God was revealed to me more. I was in ICU at the RAH when the chaplain of the school where I taught came in to see me. He prayed over me, laying on his hands, and reminded me of James 5:15 "and the prayer offered in faith will make the sick person well."

God restored me to life, from near death, and laid His healing hand on me. I relied on Him entirely, and He did not leave me or let me down.

I am so thankful for all He has done for me. Even though I am not physically the same as I was before the accident, I knew God was continuing his promise to look after me.

Luke 18:27 "What is impossible with men, is possible with God."

While I was in Julia Farr, a rehabilitation centre, I wrote a passage which summarises my feelings at that time. (1996). I quote it here –

Courage and Faith

"My Life has become a task of courage and perseverance which I try to live with much happiness. I want to show others that I am able to be courageous, and persevere towards my goal of being warden of myself. I have had a very strong faith in God who has helped me to overcome my problems, and for my family who too have stood by me courageously.

My courage has made me determined to succeed and I hope I can achieve this. My aim is to be a person who can show others how to persevere and try to be courageous when they have some trouble or an accident. I had an accident, and now I can't do some things, but I am able to write about courage and perseverance. We can make the best out of a situation by being courageous and my strong faith that God will look after me. We can make ourselves courageous by being more positive in our daily race with life and try to be more masterful in all we do, when we make many decisions. I have tried to be courageous when I have had to have operations and injections, so I know my limitations and difficulties when I have any trouble. My main aim is to encourage others to not give up when things are not going well. We must continue with more courage because we can do all things through Christ who strengthens me. (Philippians 4:13)."

After I came home from Julia Farr in 1998, I was able to go to church every Sunday with my parents. From 2002, during the week, I went to BFS with Penny, who encouraged me to share my faith with others there. I have

Acknowledgements

enjoyed it very much, over all these years – at least 14 years. God has made His promises clear to me.

Matthew 28:20 "Surely I will be with you always until the end of the age."

I have had many ups and downs, many operations and disappointments, but God has always been there holding my hand. My situation hasn't really changed much, but I know I can trust in God through all adversity, as well as in the many good times when wonderful things happen.

One of the greatest things has been the completion of my Master's degree in Musicology, from Adelaide University. I was determined to do it, and it took me eight long years to complete. This psalm was very special to me: Psalm 37:4 "Delight yourself in the Lord and he will give you the desires of your heart." Some of my favourite verses from the Bible are quoted above.

John 3:16 "For God so loved the world that He gave his one and only son, *that whoever believes in Him shall not perish but have eternal life."* This is the reason for this testimony.

During my recovery, and subsequent daily life I lean on the steadfast love of God. Jeremiah 33:3 "Call to Me and I will answer you", and He is close to me as "His compassions fail not. They are new every morning: great is thy faithfulness". Lamentations 3:22-23.

Airlie Jane Kirkham October 2016

Music Stirs my Soul

SECTION ONE

Passion

Section One
Passion

To Music..7
Music is the Beat....................................9
My Heart Rejoices...................................11
Images of Music.....................................13
Music Today..15
Minuet au Nouveau Classique..........................16
Menuet in G..17
Anecdote...18

SECTION ONE

To Music

Music stirs my soul,
uplifts a mournful mood,
expresses feelings
of the innermost being;
compassion, thought,
the rhythm of life.

Music leads me
down life's path,
roads full of meaning,
people, places.

Music interprets a person's soul;
moods, desires created
by a passing glimpse of life
in all its modes.

Music inspires,
a ruffled spirit soothed,
a frayed temper mellowed.
A heart rejoices, is happy.

Music enlivens the day.
When I hear Bach,
I feel very enlightened.
Mozart gives me feelings
of refinement.

Music makes me happy.
I am keen to hear music
at any time.
Praise God with music.
Sing songs in exaltation.
Most of all, thank God
for His gift to us.

Music will live within me forever

SECTION ONE

Music is the Beat

Music,
the beat of my existence,
the rhythm of my being,
a melody of my life
in harmony with my soul.

Music, loved with all my heart,
shows feelings,
moods, wishes, desires.
We will make music whenever we can.

My masterful memory of masterpieces,
composers of a previous age,
Pachelbel, Bach,
Verdi, Mozart,
Beethoven, Mahler -
many fine composers of music
for the people of the day.

Modern ones,
Elgar, Britten,
even the Beatles,
gave us music,
made for listening,
making us aware
of the beauty of sound.

"MUSIC",
the word which makes
my heart beat with joy.

SECTION ONE

My Heart Rejoices

When music is played,
my heart rejoices.
Music calms at all times.
Rejoice and be happy.

Music enlivens the day.
When I hear Bach,
I feel enlightened.
Mozart gives me feelings of refinement.

Beethoven stirs the passions within me,
Mahler makes me passionate and strong.
Elgar rouses feelings
of England, my heritage,
of my great love of this fine land.

Britten is my favourite composer, of modern times.
He brings great lyrical beauty to music
and a diversity of harmonies
which enrich my soul.

Music is above all an epitome of life
in passing generations;
of styles, genres, of sounds,
and masterful performances.
Music will live with me forever.

SECTION ONE

Images of Music

Music makes images
of favourite places.
Ambience remembered
of that uplifting concert.

Music everywhere:
under a tree, by the river,
listen to the sounds
tingling in the sun.

Radio plays music
non-stop classics.
Singers well known
heard with eager ears.

The opera performance
significant, unbelievable,
interpretations unique.
Sounds invade all facets of life.

The baby with her rattle.
or a night-time lullaby.
A schoolgirl learning piano,
her first instrument.

The school band plays imaginatively.
Scholars perform the old masters,
as well as new, to everyone.
Music replenishes the whole being.

SECTION ONE

Music Today

I hear music
streaming from my radio,
spinning from CDs.

Short and sweet,
Or dramatic and robust
like cascades in a valley.

A kaleidoscope of colour
all day long.
Music fills my dreams of lands afar.

Composers modern
and of yesteryear.
Sounds are amazing,

Intriguing, curious,
Staccato-like or cantabile.
Music fills my soul.

I linger with it in my thoughts,
My mind is awash
In a wonderland of music.

Minuet au Nouveau Classique

Piano

To Mrs Pamela M. Kirkham - My first copy of my first composition
with the compliments of the composer

Airlie Jane Kirkham

3 September 1985

SECTION ONE

Menuet in G

Piano

Airlie Kirkham

Anecdote

In 2002, 10 years after my accident and rehab, I expressed my wish to return to Music studies at Elder Conservatorium. An appointment was made to meet Charles Bodman Rae, Elder professor of Music.

When Charles arrived to discuss this with me, I became rather anxious while waiting.

Charles noticed this and said to me, "Airlie, I haven't come to tell you IF you can resume music studies. Rather, I want to discuss with you how you can make this possible. You have perfect pitch I've noted, and this is a great asset you have, particularly for aural work". So, I was able to enrol – my dream came true.

After coming home from an evening ASO concert, Mum asked me how it went. I replied," The tenor horn was out of tune again!!"

Airlie has Perfect pitch, and can tell you the name of any note just by its sound.

SECTION TWO

Concerts and Operas

Section Two
Concerts and Operas

An Opera House. 21

The Concert Hall. 23

Mahler in Concert. 25

An Afternoon with Airlie. 27

Thank You. 29

Japanese Song – Trio – Full Score. 30

Japanese Song – Piano. 31

Model of a Not-So-Modern Mother. 32

La Boheme. 33

SECTION TWO

An Opera House

This opera house is mighty
in ambience.
Majestic ceilings,
Gold leaf, chandeliers,
elegant pillars supporting
numerous ornate galleries.

The chorus waits in the wings.
The orchestra tunes to the oboe,
the master of wind, and the
violins are poised, hushed
by the imminent arrival of their conductor.

Success starts backstage.
Timing is everything:
sets workable, props at hand,
scenery and complex lighting,
costumes donned by soloists,
lined up backstage, awaiting cues.

Sighting "Special Stars",
Sutherland, Bonynge, Sills and Pavarotti,
temperamental Callas,
Domingo and many others.

The performance begins.
With eager ears and eyes
we consume with passion
the tragedy of La Bohème,
the fiery temperament of Lucia,
the comedy of The Magic Flute.

I recall a back stage meeting with
Domingo in Covent Garden, London.
The crush of the crowd beckoning
for his pen on my program.
Success! And it started backstage.

The opera house is my home.
Time spent in the company of the
Masters produces feelings and emotions
but its real world is behind scenes

SECTION TWO

The Concert Hall

Resounding acoustics,
majestic ceilings,
the concert hall mighty
in ambience.
Gold leaf,
chandeliers,
pillars elegant.

The grand piano stands
resplendent on stage.
The orchestra awaits its leader,
tuning to the magnificent
sound of the oboe,
the master of wind.

The audience awaits
the first melodious sound,
like an expectant father.
Violins poised,
hushed by the arrival of the leader.

The program begins.
With eager ears
we consume with passion
the elegance of Mozart,
the splendour of Mahler,
the verve of Prokofiev.

The concert hall is my home.
I love its feelings,
its emotion,
its masterful command of time,
time spent in the company
of the masters.

SECTION TWO

Mahler in Concert

Mahler's Fifth, the program cites,
a sprawling opus, intricate in design,
vast and intense.

The concert opens.
Mozart in concerto,
intended as Mahler's forerunner,
steals the show.

Dark pulsating sounds,
a prelude, unexpectedly
providing inspiration
and scintillating ambience.

Reviews in awe of the pianist —
distinctive sounds, though gloomy,
multidimensional, yet personal.
Emotional, complex,
it probes my inner being.

We pause for rest.
Do they leave the best to last?
But wait!

Majestic, magnificent Mahler
gloomy and funereal;
a powerful voice,
stormy and turbulent,
molds my impressions;

The brass distinguished and in tune.
The conductor notable
for producing fine playing.

The program inspires a combination
of genres.
Mahler gets my vote.

SECTION TWO

An Afternoon with Airlie.

Concert held at St. Columba's Anglican Church, Hawthorn, on Sunday May 21st, 2000.

The concert was arranged by several old Scholars of Woodlands to raise money to assist Airlie to purchase a speaking machine, a Delta Talker.

The programme opened with Mozart's popular oboe quartet with strings. Paul Miller (oboe) showed a brilliant technique in the opening movement. The leader, Margaret Blades, led the group with verve. The second movement was sensitive and emotional, displaying the oboe's fine command of the lower register. The finale, in the form of a rondeau, deserved the strong applause.

In between musical items, Meg Skuce read excerpts from Airlie's anthology of poetry. These outstanding readings added a spiritual and emotional dimension to the afternoon.

Vivaldi's contribution, written when he was master in charge of music at a girl's school in Venice, was the splendid concerto for four violins played by four Woodlands old scholars who are also members of the Adelaide Symphony Orchestra. The Madrigal for violin and viola by Martinu was followed by two duets, Waltz in A major (Levitsky) and the Jamaican Rumba (Benjamin)arranged for two violins.

The programme concluded with Bach's oboe and violin Concerto BWV 1060 in C min, derived from a lost work often played by two claviers. The ensemble was magnificently directed by Margaret Blades, violin, with Paul Miller, oboe, Danielle Jaquillard, Julie and Jenny Newman, violin, Cecily Matthews, viola, and Alison Miller, cello.

The ambience of the church setting, together with the audience of supportive friends, made the afternoon most successful and inspirational.

Airlie Jane Kirkham, June 2000

SECTION TWO

Thank You

Airlie wrote this poem as a thank you response to the concert at St. Columba's.

I thank you sincerely for your performance today.
Superb music.
Fine performance.
Splendid ambience.

Many kind friends, listeners who
appreciate string music.
Mozart my love,
the organ resplendent,
the oboe supreme.

A day of togetherness,
good company.
Words of emotions,
our hearts full of poetry.

My dream is being realised.
I thank God –
Soon I will be master
of my own communication.

Japanese Song

Airlie Kirkham

SECTION TWO

Japanese Song

Piano

Airlie Kirkham

Model of a Not-So-Modern Mother

From Pirates of Penzance - Act 1: A modern Major General.
Written for her mother on her Birthday
(With apologies to Sir W. S. Gilbert)

You are the very model of a not so modern mother
You've information acquired, unrivalled by any other,
You know the ways of children and you stop the fights 'tween siblings,
They may be real terrors but you still call them in order categorial,
You're very well acquainted too with all matters scholastical,
You understand teenage fads, both the simple and fanatical,
About acne and what to wear you're teeming with a lot o' news –
But sadly lacking in the facts about the latest style in shoes.
You're very good at music and you keep us at our practice,
You can play the organ; you've even tried to teach your husband, Les;
In short, in matters conjugal, you are not peered by another,
You are the very model of a not so modern mother.

SECTION TWO

La Boheme

in London

In 1987, we travelled to London for a holiday. I stayed at Earl's Court accommodation while Mum and Dad toured by car around France. I spent two whole weeks going to opera theatre productions.

When they returned, they were going to catch the tube, and met me as I rushed back to the hotel. I wasn't interested to stop and talk to them then as I had to get back to the hotel and dress for the evening opera at Covent Garden. "I've got another opera ticket for tonight", I said, and I'll be late if I don't get back". They weren't impressed!

The next day I got up early to catch the first tube at 6.00am to Covent Garden to join the queue for the cheap PROMS opera tickets. I was less than 100 persons from the first one in the queue so it looked promising. I met some lovely German girls there and talked to them about the performance. Mid-morning, Mum and Dad arrived to see how I was doing. I was so cold and hungry they went straight back to get warmer clothing and returned with some lunch.

The tickets were to see Placido Domingo singing in La Boheme. Later they brought me some tea and the German girls persuaded Mum to stay in the queue and get a ticket too. Disgruntled Dad went back to the hotel, as he didn't want to sit on the floor all evening.

It was a great opera and afterwards, I said to Mum," We can't go straight back as I am going to the stage door to queue up to get Domingo's autograph. We were first at the door but with the crowd swelling and pushing as we waited. When the burly doorman opened the stage door to let us go in, he said twelve persons for first group. I was number twelve by then and Mum number thirteen. But Mum, not wanting to let me out of her sight, slipped under his large armpits and shoulders, and said, "She can't go without me', and followed me in.

We finally caught the last tube back to our hotel by 2.00am.

A half-asleep Dad said when we arrived, "Why are you so late?"

SECTION THREE

Sounds of Music

SECTION THREE

Sounds of Music

River Sounds around the Paths. 37

Christmas Day. 38

Bells. 39

Morning Lark. 40

The May Queen. 41

Folk Dancing in the Abbey Books. 42

The Church View. 45

Memorials in Light. 47

Unseen Memories. 49

Loch Lomond. 51

Sounds of Birds. 53

Sounds of Creatures. 54

SECTION THREE

River Sounds around the Paths

Raindrops fall from trees,
leaves tremble in the wind.
Silence is broken.

Reflections rippling,
river murmurs quietly,
startled birds fly off.

Cyclists whizz along,
crickets singing break the calm.
Is there ever silence?

Christmas Day

We celebrate Christmas
with Joy and Love.
Our Saviour's Birth
is the message of the dove.

Bells are ringing
the song of Joy
Choirs are singing
of the new-born boy.

We go to church
to make our prayers,
to sing of Love
our Father has shared.

Now we rejoice,
His Son has come.
Once more we celebrate
what our Father has done.

SECTION THREE

Bells

Bells ring for many things,
part of our life,
our heritage,
communicate messages.

Foretell of doom,
danger imminent?
Rejoice with all.
What do they say?

Fire bells, church bells,
calls to worship,
dinner bells.
Lost without them?

Muffled bells,
drone bells,
glockenspiels,
carillons, school bells.
What do they tell us?

Concert bells,
interval is over.

Bells on animals,
cats and cows.
Will we find them?

Cathedral bells
peal out on Christmas day,
joyous with all people
at the Saviour's birth.

A bell at Bethlehem?
No! A star tells us.

Morning Lark

Morning Lark, that's me.
I love to wake early.
You will hear me singing
any time after three.

At night I fall asleep
in my chair before the TV,
but early in the morning,
I come alive at three.

Airlie J. Kirkham 18-7-99

SECTION THREE

The May Queen

May Day, May Day,
a celebration, an ancient custom.
Spring festival, joyful dancing
around the maypole.
Bells brilliantly belling.

Bouncing on ankles,
young persons processing
through their village,
to the May Queen Crowning
in honour of Flora.*

May Day is here.
Bouncing, bowing, bending
beneath the turning maypole,
like an amazing jigsaw coming together.
The children move frolicking,
wearing flowers, singing
the true meaning of May Day.

Flora, Roman Goddess of Flowers

Folk Dancing in the Abbey Books

Folk dancing is an integral and pivotal part of Abbey life and activities in the Abbey Books. From the very first book, Elsie J Oxenham wove her stories around the Hamlet Club established in "The Girls of the Hamlet Club" which was established by the girls of the school. As they met in Cicely's barn at Darley's Bottom, they wrote up rules for the club, and activities for all its members. They enjoyed dancing and from this grew their desires to try out all the popular dances of the time. The girls of the club practised and learnt the steps and movements of many folk dances, Morris dances and maypole dances.

Folk dancing was an old English tradition dating back many centuries, and but at the time Elsie was writing her books, Cecil Sharp had become a prominent Englishman who researched and promoted traditional dances. In 1911 Sharp founded the English Folk Dancing Society which expanded into the English Folk Dance and Song Society by 1932. Not all later critics praised his work and there has been much controversy on the source of many of his songs. However, he did unwittingly influence Elsie J Oxenham who used folk dancing as a central theme in her Abbey stories.

Interestingly, Cecil Sharp came to Australia, in particular South Australia, in 1882. During his time here he worked as a clerk in the Commercial Bank of S.A. In 1884 he became associate to the Chief Justice, Sir Samuel Way, in Adelaide until 1889, when he resigned. He had become assistant organist at St. Peter's Cathedral in1882 -3 and conducted several choral societies and the Adelaide Philharmonic. He studied law and also became director of the Adelaide College of Music to 1891. He decided to go back to England in 1892, where he continued to write music and songs as he had done in S.A. He subsequently took up a number of musical posts in England, he published folk music, and became interested in the folk music of the British Isles. He collected folk songs from 1903 and used these songs to

SECTION THREE

rescue the English folk song. He also became interested in the English folk dance, including Morris dances. He published many more dances and this led to the revival of the traditions.

Some of the first dances the hamlet club learnt were Laudnum Bunches, Rigs O' Marlow, Constant Billy, Trunkles, Country Gardens, Shepherds' Hey, Blue Eyed Stranger, The Old Mole, Newcastle and Early One Morning. More challenging dances involving more couples or sets were explored. In Chapter xvii of 'Girls of the Hamlet Club' the girls discuss learning these dances. In the next chapter they try others: Sir Roger, Gathering Peascods, Rufty Tufty and eventually Maypole dancing. Later favourites were Sellenger's Round (The Abbey Girls chapter x). Haste to the Wedding, Picking up sticks, Strip the Willow, The Eightsome Reel, If all the World were Paper and the Circassian Circle. There are far too many to enumerate them all.

Dancing requires music, and the Hamlet Club provided that too, with Margia Lane on violin, Miriam singing the songs that went with the dances, accompanied by piano. Later characters in the stories, such as Joy and Jen who were musicians, also contributed. Dancing took place at a large number of Hamlet meetings and on the occasion of a Queen being crowned.

Music for Rufty Tufty, Picking up Sticks, and Sellenger's Round is included, with instructions for the movements for Rufty Tufty. The key chosen is important too in the character of the dance.

Rufty Tufty is in the Key of G: Picking up Sticks in D minor and Sellenger's Round is Key G. More so, YouTube can be searched for videos demonstrating these dances if you should wish to try them out.

The Folk Dancing Society founded by Cecil Sharp celebrated its 90th anniversary in June 2020.

References: www.britannia.com; www.en.m.wikipedia.org

Girls of the Hamlet Club by E.J. Oxenham The Abbey Girls by E.J. Oxenham

Cecil Sharp born 2 November 1859 Died 23 June 1924. Aged 65 years

Rufty Tufty

1651 Square
Ed. 1 2 Couples Facing
G Major 3 x AABBCC

I.

A1 1-4: Meet all a Double and back.

SECTION THREE

The Church View

The shades outside keep off the sun,
redolent of that first service
under a ship's sail
brought from the port in 1836.

Inside we contemplate the memory
of the early pioneer's display
on white wall plaques.
The scene is set for us.

The organ reverberates with magnificent tones
commanding the chancel
as the golden eagle looks sternly from the lectern
at the carved wooden pews.

The great leadlight, stained-glass window
in translucent colours depicts St. Paul and the
    apostles
praising the risen Christ seated on his heavenly
    throne.
The archway states the beauty of the earth in its
    holiness.

But time has brought change —
different cultures now meet inside,
and under the sails.
Mandarin mingles in conversations
with English, or African dialects,
while children run boisterously around the grass.

SECTION THREE

Memorials in Light

Filtered light in church, no shade,
falls on marble plaques lining our church walls,
stories of our foundation fathers,
famous names honoured.
Each one stands proudly above the family pew
rented by the city's aristocracy in colonial days.
What stories they could tell.

Light falls on Hurtle Fisher, 'Buffalo' immigrant,
inaugural mayor of Adelaide, two affectionate
    children.
In charity, hope and faith John Bagshaw departed this
    life.
Unfortunate Arthur Gell lost his life at sea,
while William Bartley lost his wife Sarah.
Governor Gawler honoured his mother Julia,

Torrens, Hutt, Grote and Gouger,
Gilles, Sturt, Morphett, Angas,
Pascoe St. Léger Grenfell and trustee Gilles,
Beaumont Howard, Farrell and Reid
pastors of the church:
Pioneers revered and acknowledged
as members of the church.

In the rear, light focuses on the font,
and dapples across the ten commandments.
Windows display light, while the vestry window
links with England 1836.
Centenary window celebrates first one hundred years
beside three chancel windows.

Where there is light, there is no shade.
Outside, light and shade dance across falling
    buttresses.
Light falls on golden limestone
of the early church, newly erected, now weathered,
colonial Gothic in design, unpretentious.
The clock, transported by the 'Buffalo', is illuminated.
The bell ringing
signals the commencement of a service.
Today light shines forth from the church proclaiming
    the gospel all to see.

SECTION THREE

Unseen Memories

Slipping from the edge of the city
I come upon the mountains,
tinged blue, misty, inviting.
I wander under a rainforest roof
like a tunnel in the mountain,
unseen by the eyes until it is chanced upon.
The path takes me along in silent steps,
in wonderment, as the light filters through the deep
    gully
revealing secrets well hidden.
Fungus peeks out of undisclosed holes.
I come upon a sparkling cascade.
Behind it, a secluded gem, a cave,
a place of shared secrets: of ancient origins from
    Gondwana.
Wonders, what history, what stories would it tell.
Droplets drip in a silver stream, staccato like.
That cascade then creeps down the gully over rolling
    stones,
denuded rocks, mossy crevices, craggy cliffs,
    sandstone boulders.
I find a secret place, a pool left deep from receding
    flood waters.

Music Stirs my Soul

A bird finds its voice, a single voice choir,
a grey shrike thrush in melodious flute-like song.
Fairy wrens join in with answering trills a Capella.
The trees whisper, the grasses dance in the wind.
I linger, stand silently in this gully of long dreaming.
Spellbound, I confine these gems to my deepest
   dreams
before these moments slip away.

Airlie Jane Kirkham 2019

SECTION THREE

HAIKU

The Haiku is a Japanese style of poetry, originating from the 13th century.
It focuses on images from nature and emphasises simplicity.

First line has 5 syllables.
Second line has 7 syllables.
Third line has 5 syllables.

Sounds of Birds

Baby magpies
Share voices with mynas
Not indifferent

A bell bird calling
Echoing over the river
No one answers

Rivers slowing down
Wildlife has disappeared
Trees are crying leaves

Lorikeets screaming
Pecking fruit tree fruits and flowers
Well fed, no voice left

SECTION THREE

Loch Lomond

Traditional
Arranged by Airlie Kirkham
1988

Music Stirs my Soul

Birds fluttering
Listening to the silence
Whistle of spring

Sounds of Creatures

Sounds move upon the waters
Bees humming, murmuring.
Single melody

Dragonflies skimming
Moving along to music
over the water

The wind is crying
Frogs croaking one summer's night
Is there a clear moon?

Water rat.
Waterway forager
Summer night under moon

Scenes at the markets
Everyone is sightseeing
Piercing voices shout

SECTION FOUR

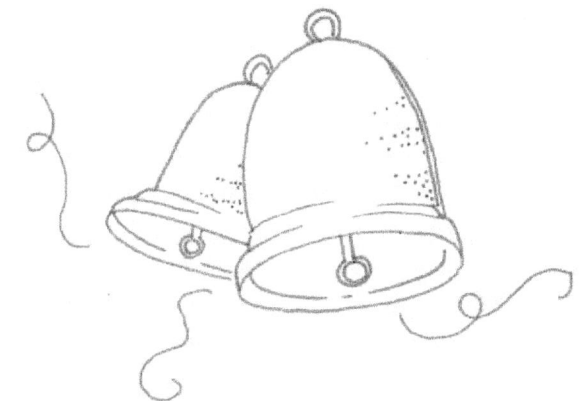

Poems and Music

Section Four
Poems and Music

Airlie's Invention 57

My Scholarship 58

My Destiny 59

Ode to Letho 60

Two Part Invention 61

Master of Music 62

Graduation Day 2/08/05 63

Two Part Invention 65

My OPERA Programmes 66

The second Program Opera in England 68

"Princess Airlie" 69

Funeral March Score 70

Charles Bodman Rae 71

SECTION FOUR

Airlie's Invention

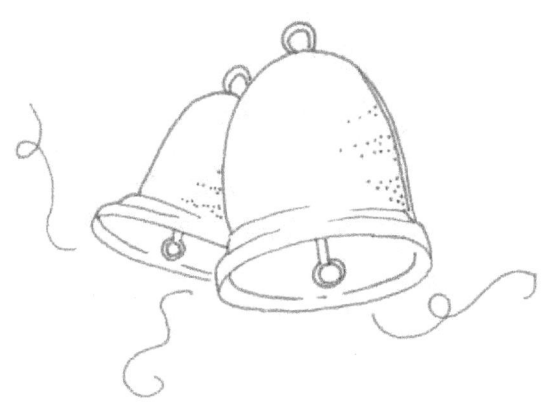

"An invention is a title used by J.S.Bach for 2-part pieces in contrapuntal style for the clavier (old piano)."

My Scholarship

Success in many forms,
is fantastic.
My future is assured.
Academia is my 'forte'.

Knowledge, understanding,
Write scintillating papers,
Bonython Hall resplendent in style,
urge me on to success.

Planning, perseverance,
modern technology,
assistive techniques,

part of my dream, my vision.
I'm there now in its midst.

Airlie J Kirkham Feb 2006

SECTION FOUR

My Destiny

It is an enigma,
a mystery, a curiosity.
My mind cannot escape my feelings.
Locked away in two persons
is my destiny.

I tried so hard.
All consuming,
   paper and pen
disseminated my thesis
for what seemed an eternity.

My mind is all consumed
with nothing else.
Will I be successful?
May I hope to win
this passion for my life?

Ode to Letho

I wonder why I was so lucky,
For someone, unknown to me at first,
to stop by me, and express with me
A love we now share, of 'bel canto'.

This was a special time of sharing.
Fortuitous, unplanned, but meant to be.
A helpmate in a vast wilderness of
Potential providers.

Amanuensis and encourager
How thankful I am.

SECTION FOUR

Two Part Invention

Piano

Airlie Kirkham
2/11/88

Master of Music

Words are not enough.
Aural appreciation,
intense listening with an ear on edge,
acutely, purposely,
playing the melody in my mind.

Sounds pitched accurately
determine the outcome.
Opera stars, divas
the bathroom tenor
must all strive for perfection.

They are the masters,
of style, of pitch, of timbre, of genre,
not the mere observer
who analyses their performances.

A mere mortal becomes a master
by masterful words,
but the true master is the one
who engages the world.

SECTION FOUR

Graduation Day
2/08/05

My dream is real.
The day has come
to give me honour
and success.

It was a dream from long ago,
impossible at first.
No way, they said,
but defying the odds
I trod a steady path forward.

Admittedly it took longer
than for those who walk on feet,
while I who walk on wheels
rolled slowly on.

Hard work, much reading,
more writing, but I did not
give up.
Now the time draws near.
What honours will I get?

Music Stirs my Soul

I have proved my critics wrong.
I have succeeded
with the help of my right hand,
my mother, who stood by me
and encouraged from behind.

Resplendent in cap and gown,
bright green and black hood for music.
I will not forget this day.
Honours Musicology,
my heart's desire.

Airlie Jane Kirkham

SECTION FOUR

Two Part Invention

Piano

Airlie Kirkham

My OPERA Programmes

In 1988, Airlie participated in the Music degree unit to conduct Radio programmes on the University radio station, 5UV. They were an hour long each week of both semesters. She chose Opera subjects to structure each programme:

Bel Canto Opera and Opera in England are two of the programmes, but all the others were on different Opera topics.

Bel Canto

1. 1. Lucretia Borgia – Donizetti. 2 acts 1803 Sung in Italian
2. Rossini: Semiramide: Let your Heart, 2 acts 1823. Sung in Italian
3. 3. Don Pasquale Act.3: Donizetti. 1843. Sung in Italian
4. Vincenzo Bellini:
   La Somnambula: 1827 –
   Love duet-Take the Ring.
   Casta Diva Norma 1831, 2 acts Italian
5. Don Pasquale: Aria 'So anchio la virtu magica'
6. Lucretia Borgia: Lucretia - Aria
7. Una Furtiva Lacrima: L'elisir d'Amore
   Donizetti 1832 Italian

Casta Diva and Una Furtiva Lacrima were the two Arias Airlie chose to study in depth when she completed her Master of Music Degree in 2010, and showed her love of this genre of opera.

SECTION FOUR

Her thesis topic was:

An Aural analysis of Bel Canto Traditions and interpretations as preserved through selected recordings.

The second Program
Opera in England

1. Music: Purcell Dido and Aeneas. 'The Faerie Queen' 1692 Sung in English
2. Handel: Acis and Galatea. A pastoral Opera Engllsh1739, 2 acts
3. The Aria: Music and its definition
4. Talk: Ballad Opera. English type of comic opera
    Popular Tunes
5. Music: Beggar's Opera – John Gay, 3 acts 1728 English
6. Talk: Thomas Arne - "Alfred" the Great
    This talk has song – "Rule Britannia" – in it.
7. Artaxerxes Music: "O too Lovely" 2 acts 1762. Talk
8. Music: Pirates of Penzance: 1879 Comic opera 2 acts. D' Oyley Carte Opera –
    "Poor Wandering One" – Mabel and chorus.
    Sung in English
9. Vaughan Williams. English composer. "The Pilgrim's Progress', 4 acts 1951, English
10. Britten: Music in Gloriana, 1953 English. Elizabethan atmosphere – QE II coronation.

SECTION FOUR

"Princess Airlie"

(With apologies to W.S.Gilbert.)
A parody of a song in "Princess Ida".
Written on a Mother's Day Card in 1986
Dear Mum, Happy Mother's Day, Love from Airlie

Airlie was a twelvemonth old
Twenty years ago!
She was quite a task, I'm told
Twenty years ago.
Her mother as well a housewife
Argues ill for a quiet life,
Baleful prophecies were rife,
Twenty years ago!

Still, she was a tiny child,
Twenty years ago!
Her mother's life was never mild,
Twenty years ago!
Now nearly twenty-one, it's true,
She's already a B.A. like you.
False and foolish prophet you.
Twenty years ago!

Funeral March Score

SECTION FOUR

Charles Bodman Rae

Sir Thomas Elder Professor of Music
MA(Cantab.) DMus (Adel) PhD. DMus (Leeds) ARCM, FCLCM.
Conservatorium of Adelaide University.

Memorial service at Holy Trinity Church, Adelaide 22 June 2022.

One of our dearest alumnae, Airlie Kirkham B.A. (English and Japanese); Diploma of Education (Sec); B.Mus.; B.Mus. Hons.; M.Mus. has just passed away at the age of 56.

From her mid-twenties, when she was a teacher at St Peter's Collegiate Girls' School, she was quadriplegic, confined to a wheelchair, after a severe car accident. Despite this, in 2010 she completed an M.Mus. dissertation on Italian Bel Canto (her wonderful mother, Pamela, serving as amanuensis). The topic of her Thesis was:

An Aural analysis of Bel Canto Traditions and interpretations as preserved through selected recordings.

After graduating with her M.Mus. she continued to attend our weekly postgraduate seminars and took a keen interest in our many doctoral projects as they developed. She wanted to embark on a Ph.D. project of her own, but it would have been "a bridge too far".

The late Airlie Kirkham wrote and published, with her mother's assistance as amanuensis, two books: one about her "locked in" condition "There is a Light at the End of the Tunnel" 2017, and the other a collection of Poems, titles, "A Kaleidoscope of Paintings" 2020.

The power of music is one of the themes resonating through her poetry. Airle was an inspiration to all, not letting any hurdle get in her way to always be a part of music which she loved so much.

I was privileged to serve as her M. Mus. supervisor and developed great admiration for this remarkable and inspiring mother and daughter team.

"Farewell, brave Airlie."

SECTION FOUR

Airlie J Kirkham August 2010

www.ingramcontent.com/pod-product-compliance
Lightning Source LLC
Chambersburg PA
CBHW071912070526
44583CB00016B/1955